desolate places

A QUIET BRILLIANCE

the braver thing series

ON KINDLE SHORT READS

Desolate Places: Reflections of Hope in Dry Seasons is ©2020 Maranda Hope Gullett.

a quiet brilliance

PUBLISHING | EST. 2020

desolate places

Reflections of Hope in Dry Seasons

Maranda Hope Gullett

Chapter 1

Desolate can feel like an apt word to describe this year and many we have known prior. Desolate feels like the home we live in, the decoration in our houses, the lens we peer through. Loss seems to be everywhere we look. It just keeps coming.

For many of us, this year is the cherry on top of many times of desolation. We have known periods in our lives where life left us. Where joy and opportunity eluded us and we felt forsaken. Times where we knew the opposite of abundance better than we knew our own names.

We know this feeling of lack and this word, desolate, somewhere deep within. Wasteland. Barren. Not barren heights. We know barren depths. It seems many efforts to produce come up empty. It feels like failure lurks around every corner.

Desolate times, for me, can feel like hit after hit. The feeling of not being able to catch up. Catch up to the pace of life, the change. Even to catch up to my own mind, my racing heart and panicked thoughts.

Desolate can feel like disappointment, anxiety and stress. It can rear its head in our hearts and minds, even our bodies. It can feel like restlessness, even hopelessness. The fear that failure is unavoidable, and there are no good things to look forward to. Barrenness can feel like we are at the end, that there's nothing left.

Likely, the year 2020 is not your first dance with desolate. It isn't mine either. The year 2020 has taken our splendid garments of hope and excitement and clothed us instead in the shame of nakedness. No longer carrying and marked by our achievements, successes or our expectation for the future. They've been removed and cast aside. Plans cancelled. Trips postponed and then put to death altogether. Opportunities crushed instead of pursued. Strife overtaking peace for many of us. Shame covers what could have been. This year seems to have become a wasteland.

We hope we see a reckoning for those we think need one. If we are brave, we will admit we are the ones who need the reckoning this year has been. We needed this upheaval, but we're ready to get settled again. This desolation was not welcome. But we hope, and even dare to believe, we are meant to find meaning in the madness. Victory in the horrific losses.

We hope it is not all in vain. We hope the desolation crowding our schools and beaches, taking inch by inch from us, will be met with banishment and instant flourishing when the ball drops and we herald a new year together.

We know this desolate reality. We are more than acquainted now. We are great bedfellows. We are trained by the loss and lack. We are aware and familiar with the ways of desolate lands and barren expectations. This year, and others in our stories like it, have trained us well.

Every article and every news conference brings a blow of desolation to our hearts. We long for a different report. A report of hope and ending the constant calamity. The calamity we still haven't adjusted to from when winter was winding down.

We look forward to a moment when this is in the past. Injustice conquered. Disease eradicated. Deception vanquished and ended for good.

There must be an end? There must be a better side of this narrative we can't escape in this desolate year. We have hope. But, every day, there are tyrants waiting at our door to dash each one.

Perhaps you have lost a loved one this year to senseless violence, to a lifelong disease, or even to a new disease that will not loosen its grip. So much loss has been crowded out of view by dominant news cycles and reports or mayhem in our streets. Maybe you have been stuck in your home with someone who wishes you harm with their every breath and blow. Domestic violence has also risen, adding to the desolation for families, women and children.

Possibly you are one who is struggling under the weight of something that feels it is its mission to bury you. You fear being buried alive in the books, expectations and isolation. For those families treading the new rough terrain of distance learning, your homes are covered in new materials. You may work from home, along with your children, or on your own, away from the team you trusted, who trusted you. It can feel so foreign, so unwelcome. It can feel so terrifying.

Desolate may be too easy a word. Barren may be too simple. Not painful enough to describe, to name the losses.

Some knew desolate places before this year came and served us all the unexpected and drove our plans into the dirt. Some of us have known this in tastes, and some have known desolation in rivers that would not stop.

***

Desolate can be a description and an action against a place or people. It can be perpetrated against ideas and dreams. Against nations and families.

A Google search finds that desolate can be applied to a place or it can be an act perpetrated against a person or location. A place can be "in a state of dismal emptiness." We can make a person "feel utterly wretched and unhappy."[1]

Desolate is a state of existence or a crime against a person or place. We can describe both as forsaken, bare, bleak, dismal or grim.

There is nothing pleasant to be found. No fertile ground for

1. Google search for "Desolate"

life or hope where desolate has touched down or has been inflicted.

***

2020 is not the only perpetrator of desolation we have known. Each of us knows a desolate moment. A memory, an experience, a fear that stripped the joy from our eyes and pushed our faces down. We may have been terrorized by a cruel person, someone we should have been able to trust. We may have survived a natural disaster or catastrophe and had to find a way to pick up the pieces, however many there were, that remained. There are so many ways desolation can touch our lives, mare our souls, and leave us wanting and fainting.

We will all bring different notions, different preconceived ideas and memories to this word and this idea of desolation. As many as read these words are as many as the unique experiences of desolation, and more. We may not have termed our experiences desolate. We may not have identified what happened as a desolated relationship or situation. Yet, we have all been touched by lifelessness, hopelessness. These have tracked us and hunted us all our lives. 1 Peter 5:8 warns, "Your adversary the devil prowls around like a roaring lion, seeking someone to devour." It's not out of the norm to have experienced hard and painful things. We are warned in the Bible things will not always be comfortable or easy[2].

---

2. John 16:33

Desolate is not just for this year of disease and heartache; injustice and confusion. Desolate is for when we see no life. No life around us. No life in our futures. When we can't see and enjoy others and be known.

Sometimes desolate can conjure images and ideas of valleys, deserts and wastelands; the times in life we are told are best to grow in. We may expect that with loss and lack, there should be strides in growth of who we are. This idea or teaching that when things are stripped from us, it means they are removed out of our way so we will have opportunities to grow. It's a pressure to grow in some way that can be perceived and measured outwardly. This is just another device to shame us. It's one more indicator of desolation.

Desolate circumstances may trick us into times of punishing ourselves, trying to exact and squeeze out an acceptable or comforting form of personal growth and achievement. We believe we can display this and justify the loss, the dormancy. Something to justify the barrenness we feel we can't escape.

This confusion and self-inflicted punishment becomes yet another symptom of the desolation. The wasteland we find ourselves in when opportunities dry up. When friendships are lost. When we are told to stay home from work indefinitely. When disease rages against our families and communities. It's easy to pick up a banner of self-improvement. A commission of somehow overcoming something that still exists and we cannot make by sheer effort leave us alone.

You don't have to have been alive in the year 2020 to know the burden of desolate times and how they cause us to heap the unrealistic on our hearts and bodies and only add to the waste and stark landscape. It's human nature to expect more of ourselves and others than is realistic. And yet, there is a better way.

Every time and season can be fertile ground. Every time we lose, we can sink our roots in further to the Lord and His love for us that isn't shaken or moved by loss or failure. But, we must remember that as roots sink deeper, the growth will not be seen immediately. This is the beauty that can be found in desolate times. It's a beauty that doesn't flash itself around and call attention. It's a gift and an intimate journey. It's a hidden reality within the losses we see piling up.

And there is no shame. We may be hearing a lie deep in our souls that we should be ashamed for not conquering the world while we are in this desolate time. We may be hearing, or being shamed to believe, there is no better time than now to learn a new language, a new skill, to make our home perfect, and endless other pulls toward a perfect and unattainable image. But there is no shame in not producing a world of changes, growth or content right now. Any time we are trekking through a deep valley, we are not subject to the expectations of others or ourselves. We are subject to the flow of water in and through where we find ourselves.

In John 7, our Jesus calls Himself our refreshing drink. He invites us to come and get what we need from Him. He is our refreshment. Even in a valley. Even in a barren and desolate place. The waters still flow. The love still chases us into every crevice and our job in barrenness is to abide. To be. To settle in. Not to resist, but to allow our good God to be Himself, and to be our cool drink.

Psalm 23:6 says, "Surely goodness and mercy shall follow me all the days of my life..." The mercy and goodness of God follow us, chase us. As the enemy pursues us, the Love of God runs harder after us. Goodness and mercy. They don't set out to steal anything from us. They don't attempt to guilt us into a different posture or schedule. They chase us down to put us in the grace of the Father. To make us safe and well in His love.

Barrenness may tell us the story we are shut down. That things have stopped and only loss will dominate. Desolate may lie to our hearts that all is lost.

The truth is that we can stop in the slowdown. We are per-mitted in the valley, under high obstacles, to be. To rest and sink deep. The water still flows and is bringing life, and we can root into our Jesus. Shame would tell us we need to ac-complish more. But Love would tell us to be in this moment and to see the life that is meant to spring from death.

Chapter 2

Jesus never played by our rules. He never thought much of the rules of the Pharisees. He didn't seem to think much of the rules of the disciples. He was always living from somewhere else, tuned into a different way of living.

He had an innate truth that He was living by, and this was far more precious than rules. Over, and over in the Gospels we see Him frustrating the ideas of people who adored their tradition. He just couldn't stop upsetting their normal. He was trying to make them free. He was trying to help them get somewhere their rules and traditions wouldn't allow them to go.

He was trying to get them back into the Garden. The place where a way of life was supposed to come from before sin came to dominate in the place of freedom and grace.

Jesus kept trying to bring freedom and grace back to center stage. He knew how beautiful they are. He knew how they would change the makeup of humanity. They can transform everything with no value attributed to it, and make it something worth love and affection.

He wanted people who had no esteem to be overflowing with value and merit. He wanted justice and mercy to run in the streets, unencumbered. He wanted to see love lavished on all, with no parameters set for who may receive and who would have to go without.

He wanted to feed the people He was sent to. We see Him feeding those gathered around Him, far from villages and homes. We see him tend to their needs in places that were regarded as nothing. We see Him make something of what felt like overwhelming nothing.

Matthew 14:13-21 isn't the first time we see Jesus attend to hunger. It is however the first of two accounts of Him feeding men in the thousands, not counting women and children.

"Now when Jesus heard this, he withdrew from there in a boat to a desolate place by himself. But when the crowds heard it, they followed him on foot from the towns. When he went ashore he saw a great crowd, and he had compassion on them and healed their sick. Now when it was evening, the disciples came to him and said, "This is a desolate place, and the day is now over; send the crowds away to go into the villages and buy food for themselves." But Jesus said, "They need not go away; you give them something to eat." They said to him, "We have only five loaves here and two fish." And he said, "Bring them here to me." Then he ordered the crowds to sit down on the grass, and taking the five loaves and the two fish, he looked up to heaven and said a blessing. Then he broke the loaves and gave them to the disciples, and the disciples gave them to the crowds. And they all ate and were satisfied. And they took up twelve baskets full of the broken pieces left over. And those who ate were about five thousand men, besides women and children." (Emphasis added)

Jesus had a habit that I can relate with of withdrawing to have some alone time. Here in Matthew 14, he had done just that. As was normally the case when He pulled this move, people didn't really get the clue and leave Him be for a bit. They followed.

Jesus had not withdrawn to a quiet and lush place like other times. Verse thirteen tells us He purposely went to a desolate place.

We need to stop here already. Why would He purposely seek out a desolate place? Why was this on His criteria for a spot to be refreshed by some solitude? I believe we can be invited in to wonder and ponder the decisions that may seem quirky. Why was desolate, barren, uninhabited and isolated a desirable location for our Jesus to withdraw?

This is truly wonderful to pause and marvel at. He did not carry the same scorn and shame for a bleak spot on the Earth the way we do. He held a completely different view of desolate, a different belief that was, for Him, an invitation to something that could be found there. Something that could be found in desolation.

We can get a lot out of all the awkward and seemingly odd things found in the Bible. There are a lot of them. Weird little pieces of information that seem out of place or even wrong to our modern, rule-obsessed ways. But awkward and odd are not foreboding. They are intriguing, if we go a little further past our assumptions.

Here, in this verse, we can see something about our God that we don't normally look at or consider. Something that doesn't normally fit our narrative of Christian living. Desolate and barren, they are not the end. They are not to be avoided and scorned. They contain life. There is something that can thrive in them.

This is one signal among many in Matthew, Mark, Luke and John of how we are invited to view things we normally do not second guess. None of us would willingly travel by boat to a desolate place for reflection and refreshment. We would find a verdant valley. Maybe a park, waterfront bench or a quiet library. We would miss and diagnose a barren spot as an impossible choice. Our natural inclination would not be to seek out a setting of lifelessness. We would look on the outward and go another way, potentially missing something wild and life-giving.

This isn't how Jesus sees it. He makes a choice wholly unlike the ones we make every day. We go after tea and coffee to spur us on. We chase entertainment to revive us and suffer the loss of time we could have spent being truly revived by the presence of God. He chose to fast in a wilderness. He chose to rest in a desolate place.

***

The next sentence of verse thirteen tells us that crowds followed Jesus out into the desolate place. Maybe we can be like them, and not question the choice of where we can find him, and just pursue Him wherever He is going.

However, in verse fifteen, we see the disciples judge and pass a verdict on this place chosen by Jesus and the crowds. The disciples proclaim it a desolate place. A place that can carry no provision for the people that Jesus' compassion was aroused for. They needed food, and the best idea the disciples could come up with was to send them on their way.

I have done this countless times. Judged a place I was in in life or with the Lord or in a relationship. I have guessed I could find nothing nourishing, nothing of God in it, and decided that it was best to move on. I have often forsaken God in the places of my life where I could find nothing redeemable, by my own estimation. I moved on before He did. I did not get to see all He could do with a relationship. All He could do with a situation. I demanded a change of scenery. Something that appeared lush. I wanted the situation to match my understanding of God, myself, others, and even my own potential. That's the lushness I was demanding. That's called going around the mountain again. Needlessly. Repeating the same patterns and expecting growth and better things.

How quick we are, like the disciples in this situation, to declare our situations lifeless. We end the search and romance of finding Jesus everywhere we can find him. We are ready so much faster than He is to move away from something. He wants to bring life and progress and fullness through what we label as insufficient, desolate, barren and bleak. Perhaps He would want to heal, when we just want to move on and let go. We are not pleased with what the situation or relationship feels like, and so we find something that allows us to get away. To not dig deeper.

How often do we diagnose a colleague, a fellow driver on the road, a family member with something that allows us out of dealing with them? A condition or personality type that gives us permission not to try harder, find compassion and empathy in a dry relationship. We often, like the disciples on that desolate patch of Earth, put the axe to something with life in it, in our haste.

Jesus was not confused about the condition of the place He retreated to. And He respected those who followed Him. He knew they had chosen to follow the Lord. He knew the fruits of where He was. The very truth of where His feet were, and He decided that He would pull out the life contained in that desolate place.

Where the disciples wanted to send the crowds on their way to find food for themselves, Jesus wanted them to have a seat. To enjoy a seat. Most of us know the story well.

Jesus, lovingly, we assume, instructed His disciples in verse sixteen, "But Jesus said to them, 'They do not need to go away; you give them something to eat'."

I'm not sure if we can be certain how direct Jesus was being here. He may have added some flourishes to His instruction, or it could have gone down the way we read it in the English Standard Version. We see a very direct King contradict His knights and instead flip the script. We see Him, in very few words, communicate that their assessment is wrong, and instead they will get to share the joy of caring for the crowds.

They follow Jesus' instructions and gather the five loaves of bread and two fish, and get to work.

I cannot recall the last time I was in a gathering of over five thousand people. I cannot imagine how vast that amount of people would be. And this was not only five thousand people. There were many more as only the men are counted in this figure, as was custom in ancient Hebrew times. In reality, and in the grandness of this story, the five loaves and two fish fed at least ten thousand people.

This is one of Jesus' greatest miracles. It's one we all know.

And yet, it's one where we stop at feeding five thousand with five and two. We forget this happened in a desolate place that was chosen for retreat. We forget about the end of the story that opens up even more miracles for those who find themselves in desolation.

When everyone in the assembled crowd was fed, and that to the full, they gathered the leftovers. In the twentieth verse, we see "they all ate and were satisfied." From desolation and a meager offering, satisfaction resulted. An enjoyable meal was somehow prepared from barrenness and the leftovers were staggering.

Twelve basketfuls of bread and fish were gathered once every member of the crowd was full.

Pause for a moment and consider what this means for the existence this year has been for many of us. Pause and think about what the result of twelve baskets full of more food means for the lack and loss we face this year. And not just this year. Consider the implications this miracle can have on the loss you are grieving, on the job that drains your energy and inspiration, on the marriage that taxes your capacity for empathy. Consider what twelve basketfuls left over means for every desolate time in your life.

Could it be that we have misunderstood desolate?

***

Can you think of places you have deemed lifeless? I have a few that come to mind. There have been times where I have determined that God is in the wrong and I cannot find what I need from where I am currently planted. All the while, He is ready to bring life to the surface.

Sometimes a desk is a tether. A job feels like walls. Sometimes, a relationship or family matter can feel like a prison cell. Locking us into something we find no value in. It isn't exciting. It isn't producing the fruit we think should come fast enough. It isn't making us feel successful and mature.

We examine our surroundings and our options. If we declare

this place desolate, maybe our time will end soon. We cry out, Look God, nothing good can come of this. It is time to move on.

And yet, in the midst, He is seeing the life just below the dull surface. He sees the miracle and the fullness He can bring forth. Where we declared no life could exist, he feeds over five thousand precious souls from the fruits of a desolate place. And a mind-boggling amount remains to be gathered as leftovers, to continue the blessing.

In Matthew 15:32-39, we see Jesus repeat his miracle. The wild abundance of God struck again. A double whammy to yet again signal to us that the truth of Heaven is abundance.

"Then Jesus called his disciples to him and said, "I have compassion on the crowd because thy have been with me now three days and have nothing to eat. And I am unwilling to send them away hungry, lest they faint on the way." And the disciples said to him, "Where are we to get enough bread in such a desolate place to feed so great a crowd?" And Jesus said to them, "How many loaves do you have?" They said, "Seven, and a few small fish." And directing the crowd to sit down on the ground, he took the seven loaves and the fish, and
having given thanks he broke them and gave them to the disciples, and the disciples gave them to the crowds. And they all ate and were satisfied. And they took up seven baskets full of the broken pieces left over. Those who ate were four thousand men, besides women and children. And after sending away the crowds, he got into the boat and went to

the region of Magadan." (Emphasis added).

This time, the crowd had followed for days. There were just one thousand fewer men. The supplies of such a desolate place were slightly more; seven loaves and a few small fish. And our Jesus brought too much out of not enough. He knew their need and the condition they were in and not willing to leave them to languish.

This time, the leftovers would fill seven baskets. All from a desolate place. A place that could produce no life. This place, that if we had been there, we would have confirmed as dead, comfortably fed four thousand men, and the women and children in that crowd.

Could it be, desolate is not what we have believed it to be?

Chapter 3

I wonder if when Jesus saw this desolate place to retreat to in Matthew 14, or heard the pronouncement of desolation from His disciples, if He thought back to Isaiah's bold prophecy in Isaiah 43? With language and imagery such as "way in the wilderness", "streams in the desert," I wonder if the desolate condemnation wasn't the least bit intimidating for Jesus.

Jesus knew the scriptures. He knew them better than the Pharisees and believed them and could see past the words into the nature of God. He carried that very nature of God and we see Him moved with compassion repeatedly in the scriptures to provide in a dramatic and miraculous way for those who approached Him in need.

Jesus would have known the prophet Isaiah's words very well. He quoted them many times in the gospels. This passage in particular, I wonder if He would have recalled it when the disciples claimed they were in a desolate, and therefore lifeless spot.

Isaiah 43:16 proclaims that the Lord makes a way in the sea, a path in the mighty waters. God makes ways to travel and move about with freedom amid overpowering circumstances. He creates a road to walk on, where none existed before. He could make a way through a barren land to provide for

His people.

"I will make a way in the wilderness and rivers in the desert", is declared in Isaiah 43:19.

Where we, like the disciples, can see nothing redeemable or valuable about times in our lives of loss, or waiting through what seems like nothing, or the times we have survived what felt like barren wastelands; what if the heartbeat of God was to make a road right through that heat and desolation? What if in that pressure and loss we are meant to watch a pathway emerge that is forged by the goodness of God?

How many of us have been through seasons we felt that there was no way through, no end imaginable? How many of us have looked at our circumstances and have felt they reduced us to witnessing the death and loss of a relationship or opportunity to live one of our dreams? How many of us have felt the parched mouth in our body, crying and desperate for refreshing water to spring up in our midst? A wellspring of water to refresh us, a reprieve in anxiety's midst and the fear that releases in desolate times. We longed for goodness to pepper the landscape of horrible news that seemed to follow us.

Jesus knew we needed this. Our Father God knows we long and cry out for this refreshing. For this ability to see in the midst of the dust storm that the desert produces.

The God we know, the God we learn to trust more and more every day, is the God who knows how to carve out roadways to a destination in the midst of what should be wasteland. He is experienced in making the lost and ravaged places of the earth, into an oasis of His provision and goodness. He knows how to change the narrative. He knows how to bring out life and the way to move forward when all roads seem locked and we've wound up in a ditch.

***

These days, we have numerous translations at our fingertips for reading and studying the Word. There simply is no shortage of different verbiage and even spins on a verse. Reading Isaiah 43:16-21 in various translations will bring you a little more fullness of understanding of "the way" made through the wilderness.

In the English Standard Version, this passage reads "Thus says the Lord, who makes a way in the sea, a path in the mighty waters, who brings forth chariot and horse, army and warrior;
they lie down, they cannot rise, they are extinguished, quenched like a wick: "Remember not the former things, nor consider the things of old. Behold, I am doing a new thing; now it springs forth, do you not perceive it? I will make a way in the wilderness and rivers in the desert. The wild beasts will honor me, the jackals and the ostriches, for I give water in the wilderness, rivers in the desert, to give drink to my chosen people, the people whom I formed for myself that they might declare my praise."

In other translations, we find words like paths, roads, ways, course of life, mode of action. And making a way can be read as opening a way or making a pathway.

The wilderness, the desert, the barren depths we walk through in this life that carry the declaration of desolation; these places, in reality, contain the promise of God making a way. They hold the right setting for God showing up and acting powerfully to open up something for us that was not there before.

It seems we have misunderstood desolate.

***

Desolate means unlivable. It means nothing can flourish. There is no flow of life, no water to cause anything to grow. And yet, in Isaiah 43:20b God declares, "for I will give water in the wilderness, rivers in the desert." The wilderness and the desert are dried up, dead places; and these are where God intends to bring flowing sources of water. Imagine a brown landscape, stretching as far as you can see. Then the Lord brings a river right through that environment. Cutting through the brown, a sea of blue emerges. It would leave nothing untouched by life.

God had done this before for the Israelites, the people this passage is spoken over. He had made ways open where there were none for them as paths of escape from tormentors. Earlier in the Old Testament, He leads them out of Pharaoh's grasp in Egypt through the Red Sea. He opened a path right through it, dry and wide, to walk on. That path later disappeared, and the sea swallowed their pursuers.[3]

The audience for this passage in Isaiah were not unfamiliar with the miracles God could perform on their behalf. To make something that didn't previously exist, come to life for them. A way through the desert, coming into existence, just for them, was not unusual.

Many times in my life, and in the lives of my friends and family, God has provided where there was no provision possible. He is our God of the way through.

And yet, we feel the desolate times creep up and then swallow us in years like this year, and in seasons of change or loss. We feel the threat of death, loss, turmoil or upheaval. The threat to our comfort. The threat to our normal. Even the threat to our life or lives of those we care for. At times, we feel our dreams threatened. It seems they can be easily stolen, and we will be left undefended, desolate. And we forget that God is a way maker. A water and life giver. This is who He is. It's how He is.

When we read water and rivers in verse twenty, it's also speaking of streams, fountains, wells, prosperity and the creation of waterways. It's not just a river. A single source. It's a promise of many sources of refreshing, all rooted in His love and provision. This is His view of desolate and barren. These are places He loves to bring refreshing and life. I think He

---

3. Exodus 14:1-31

must love to do what we have decided does not fit or make sense.

***

The crown of this passage is nestled in the middle of it. The pinnacle of the promise and heart of God for his people is between all the verses on what His provision and way will look and feel like. In verse nineteen, He says the thing we often quote. The words we bank so many new ideas and ministries on. In this verse, He was speaking of Himself and how He would be known by His people Israel, how He can be known by us.

"Behold, I am doing a new thing; now it springs forth, do you not perceive it?"

The Israelites at the time Isaiah was speaking these words were in exile. They were in true desolation. True despondency in a foreign land. They needed refreshment, they truly needed the hope that their God would come through for them. They needed a way and a road made, out of nothing.

And God was announcing He would do just that, through very figurative and poetic language.

Even this line, "Behold, I am doing a new thing...do you not perceive it?" is figurative. Isaiah is trying to get his audience's attention. Using poetry, metaphor and language that calls back to another memory is powerful for getting an audience to notice something they may have forgotten or are trying to overlook.

The Israelites were in captivity, in exile. This is desolate. This is desperate. We can feel possessed by desolation and barren times and circumstances as well. In this verse, Isaiah is calling out. He is redirecting their attention to deliverance. He is asking that they consider it. That they allow themselves to be caught up in the promise again, to believe it is possible.

So often, we need the same. So often, I need to have someone grab me and remind me of deliverance. Remind me that my present is not permanent and has not been my forever. That is what Isaiah is doing here. He is beckoning God's kids to be possessed by something else. To be possessed by the possibility, by the desire in the Lord's heart, by His ability to bring liberty. To bring life where death is all they can see.

The invitation is to take their eyes off their suffering. Off of the insurmountable obstacle life seems to be and instead fix their gaze on the God who opened up a sea for them.

This verse, however, holds a shift. Yes, God opened a sea for them and did many more miracles as they wandered forty years in the wilderness, but He has even more up His sleeve. He can do things in fresh ways, again and again.

This call out in verse nineteen is also prophetic in nature. The Israelites are being alerted to let go of how things have happened in the past. Not to forget, but not to hold up as the only way the Lord can move. It's a call to lift their eyes to what God is already wanting to do for them. To see how He is already making a way in their midst. He intends to be their refreshing, their liberation. His plan and His way is to be their safety, home and source of rest as circumstances toss them about. As their captors pronounce desolation, God intends to be the water in their midst that can cause flourishing.

***

Desolation attempts to threaten and consume us. It attempts to dominate our view.

But we, like the Israelites, are being called too, to lift our heads, to lift our eyes and see our God standing with us. He is with us, waiting for us to give Him our attention. He wants to pour out and be the living waters we need. He is the cool drink when we are parched, the breeze that surprises us when we are languishing in the heat and the sadness. He longs to lift our heads to notice the river in the midst of His presence, person and healing.

We are beckoned to not look for the old things. The past deliverances, the past ways of God through a situation, or a tragedy. We are asked and encouraged to look up and see what He is doing now. He is moving now in our lives. In this year and on this Earth. He always has the intention to fill creation and to be our source of healing and refreshing.

It may be that He is opening up a new course of life, like other translations would call the pathway in the desert. Perhaps the new thing He is doing in our lives will require something new and bold from us. Something we have not done or tried, or even been willing to consider before. A new way of seeing people or circumstances. He could be giving us rivers in the shape of new actions at work, new habits with our spouses or children. The ways He opens for us will be new to us. He is our way through and He brings healing and growth through things we have often refused to ponder.

He knows we need to be refreshed. He knows when bareness and lifelessness strike us. He knows when we can only see the lost all around us, and His heart is set to be our source. We need not dwell on the suffering and the past methods of God. We can know Him now and see His new move on our behalf now.

Desolate doesn't have to have the last word.

Chapter 4

Let's look to one more spot in the Old Testament that shows us a different window, maybe a door so violently thrown open, the frame is destroyed; Psalm 65:9-13.

"You visit the earth and water it; you greatly enrich it; the river of God is full of water; you provide their grain, for so you have prepared it. You water its furrows abundantly, settling its ridges, softening it with showers, and blessing its growth. You crown the year with your bounty; your wagon tracks overflow with abundance. The pastures of the wilderness overflow, the hills gird themselves with joy, the meadows clothe themselves with flocks, the valleys deck themselves with grain, they shout and sing together for joy."

The dismal and deathlike times we may find ourselves in during our lives; while often horrendous, are not the ending word. Barren and desolate do not carry the day or the land we call home forward. They do not finish the story. They did not for Jesus, and they will not for us.

We've been looking at this idea of desolate through the lens of a landscape that is desolate and thought to not be able to bear fruit or life. If we can find in our lives similar circumstances that resonate as desolate and dead, then we can find and hear the hope in Psalm 65 for those landscapes.

It's never easy. We were made for the Lord and to enjoy Him as He enjoys us, and yet somehow, this is never our default. Our natural setting is more often to lean into the desolate. We usually ground down into the impossible soil of not enough and scarcity. When, in our hearts, we house the King of Kings and Lord of Lords who has, for us, an unfamiliar process for dealing with all things marked by desolation.

Let's dive into His view.

***

Psalm 65 is a place I have felt the Lord draw me to spend some time in often. And I still find it far more natural to resist and assume I know enough already, than to slow down and allow myself to find Him in the rhythms and the truth carried in these verses.

We're going to take this verse by verse, bite by bite, and search for more of the Lord's heart. We can allow the word to wash over us. We can allow the Heart of God to sink past our skin and inhibitions and really listen for His nature in each of these lines.

Verse 9, "You visit the earth and water it; you greatly enrich it; the river of God is full of water; You provide their grain, for so You have prepared it."

Take a moment. Maybe this is native for you. Maybe this

isn't, to pause verse by verse, maybe even line by line. I pause in several ways. Sometimes, I journal; sometimes I pray; sometimes I drop everything, stare at the words, then stare at the wall and consider whatever stayed in my thoughts. There's no right way to be with the Lord. There's no wrong way to wonder at Him.

If this isn't natural for you, I pray and hope some form of pausing with the Lord can become normal and fun for you. It isn't always natural for me. It's still a journey of laying down more of myself to consider more of Him. When I do this with the Lord, it becomes the best home I'll ever have. It's the safest place on Earth. It's a time to snuggle in closer to the Lord and listen to Him, like Mary did.[4] Possibly the idea of snuggling doesn't sit right for you. Being with the Lord can be a time of study, a time of prayer, worship. The ways we relate and enjoy friendships are the same ways we can enjoy time with God.

In this verse, there are so many declarative statements about the Lord's activity in the Earth. Here, we do not see a passive God who stands far away and leaves us to desolation. We see a good, kind, gracious, even fun God come close.

The language of this verse describes God almost as a gardener. An attentive and detail-oriented gardener. He has set up the earth and the grain. He has made sure there is an abundance of water. He makes sure there is not only water flowing, but access to further sources of water, the river of

4. Luke 10:39

God that overflows.

He visits. He makes it a point to be with us. Another way of looking at this might be that He checks on us, takes time to attend to us and make sure we are doing well. He longs to be trusted and be allowed in, to hear our hearts and see to our health. To make sure we know we are loved.

He enriches the soil, or the surroundings of our lives. He's wanting to make sure the substances we are drawing from in for our lives are enriched, meaning full of Him and His nature. It's the way He functions. It's the way He has prepared us to function, and the Earth. We are meant to be exposed continuously to His enriching. He is a participating God. He draws near and is involved and intent to make refreshing available.

***

The next verse is very intimate in nature. For me, it calls to the imagination a father softening the brow of his child and easing the fears and anxieties. This verse feels deeper than the words, and as though the real meaning and image of God contained therein, will take a little while for us to unpack for all it reveals.

"You water its furrows abundantly, settling its ridges, softening it with showers, and blessing its growth," Psalm 65:10.

Here we see God get a little closer. We see Him get more involved. Step deeper toward the places in this garden that need more attention. He plants not only more than enough seed, provides more than enough water and designs this garden; he checks the nooks and crannies. He attends to every spot to soften and prepare every inch for growth and love.

Imagine a loved one, an aunt, grandparent or mother, caress your check, smooth your hair back, and it immediately settles you. Your thoughts calm down, muscles release their stranglehold on your nerves, and you can relax. That's the scene we get to sink into in this verse. We get to be the ones settled and calmed. Soothed and loved deep past skin into our bones.

Desolate times in our lives make us tense. They make us grind our teeth, clench our jaws and hold on for dear life with every breath. In fact, there isn't a single breath that comes easy in desolation, in loss, in the free fall that sometimes grips us. This verse brings God closer. Our faces are held. Our concerns cared for and trusted to Him.

Then, the ending line of this verse, "and blessing its growth", is profound.

Growth is blessed. Growth is in progress. Our progress, our stretching and growing are blessed. We aren't fully grown. Our view of life and our circumstances are not fully formed. We are ever learning and developing, changing and expanding, and here we see a radical promise that this growth we'll never outgrow is blessed. It's seen. It's known. It's sacred. It's allowed to exist and continue. We don't have to be finished right now. He blesses our growth. We get to keep growing toward Him.

***

"You crown the year with Your bounty; Your wagon tracks overflow with abundance. The pastures of the wilderness overflow; the hills gird themselves with joy," Psalm 65:11 and 12.

Our good God crowns the year with bounty. His own bounty; He bestows it on our years, on our seasons. Whatever shape they are in, He comes to set His nature and ways upon them.

This language is very poetic and metaphorical. It can be a challenge for more linear and cerebral thinkers to accept and enjoy. I think in poetry, essays and lyrics, so these verses come alive in my mind. But for many, they won't. Though this passage is lyrical, a great way to find the depth is also to study the original context they are written in. If the language of these verses is hard to assimilate and to get the meaning of, study is a wonderful way of sitting with this passage and sitting with the Lord and learning more of His heart.

Bounty speaks to me of too much, more than enough, a quantity where I never have to consider need or lack. This is how God longs to interact with our times on the Earth. Giving too much, or more than enough into them. More than enough good things.

The paths of the Lord's provision are teeming with abundance. The message in verse eleven is too much. God is the

God of too much. Too much of what we need, too much love, too much provision and mercy and too much life amid whatever we face.

We can feel under attack or under the weight of scarcity and fear, disease and famine. But should we face loss, He is still the God of too much. He is still the God that makes a way for abundance and overflow, healing, restoration and growth. There is still water flowing. There are still opportunities waiting, even in this desolate time.

Desolate times cause us to miss the goodness of God that runs after us. They blind us to the way God longs to participate and move in our lives. He is the God of too much, but often, circumstances steal our attention, and we miss His wagon tracks. We miss His movements to bless and astound us. This verse pulls us to turn aside and catch what He is doing, right in the middle of hard and trying, loss and hopeless.

***

The two phrases in verse twelve hit me every time. They are odd and figurative, but thrilling in their metaphorical whimsy. "The pastures of the wilderness overflow…" How funny. The pastures, which are places of growth and unending life, in the wilderness, a place thought to be desolate and barren, overflow. These two do not seem to belong together. But the Psalmist combines them to speak of the Lord's nature. The Lord's confounding, abundant heart. He creates too much in places where we expect there to be nothing. He puts structures that contain life in places we think are dead. He creates belonging between two things we never imagined belonging together. And then he crowns it with abundance. The God of too much.

The next line of this verse starts a little refrain of seeing the inanimate behave like living things. Once again, the language can seem a little odd, but there are aspects to glean and help us understand our God better.

"The hills gird themselves with joy." Girding oneself is to put on a belt or to secure something to your person. The hills go about girding themselves with joy. What can this mean for us? What can this mean for the Earth we walk on and the way we can interact in life?

Hills are securing joy to themselves. We can be instructed, encouraged, and given hope that we can do the same. We can walk about and secure, attach and keep joy on us. This is a provision in the nature of the Lord, to be knitted with joy in this life. Joy is the confidence in the Lord that He has us and what concerns us secure and taken care of. And though, yes, it does not always feel that way; the truth is we can trust Him like the wilderness in this verse is trusted to Him, to be clothed in abundance.

There are many instances, particularly in the New Testament, where believers are instructed to wear a characteristic of the Lord; put on love, put on the armor of God, and so on.[5] Putting on, or wearing, some trait of the Lord is not rare or

5.Ephesians 6:11

38

unusual. It is a commonly encouraged aspect of our life of faith in God.[6] We can believe that He is good and to allow His finished work of the cross to mean that we can be like Him. And we can even figuratively dress like Him and be like Him more and more in His nature and how He treated others and the Earth.

The next verse will take us a little further into this perhaps odd practice. It would not have been odd for Jesus. He would have been familiar with the Hebrews scriptures and would have known these verses and the ideas of the Earth crying out in praise and trust in God. Jesus would have been comfortable with the figurative and poetic nature of the Hebrew scriptures, as that was one of the dominant forms of writing in them.

***

Verse thirteen further introduces an idea of belonging.

"The meadows clothe themselves with flocks; the valleys deck themselves with grain, they shout and sing together for joy," Psalm 65:13.

Flocks belong with meadows. Grain is meant to exist with valleys where water is flowing in to sustain the growth. And both meadows and valleys, adorned as they are meant to be, join in praise.

6.Colossians 3:9, 10, 13, 14; Isaiah 61:3; Galatians 3:27; 1 Peter 5:5

The meadow gathers and brings to itself flocks to graze and be taken care of within its borders, and from its bounty. Such a wild relationship we see here. These two aspects of nature belong together.

A valley is at its best when grain is flourishing. A valley is truly a valley when it supports the abundance of grain. These two belong together and work well together.

We can say the same for us. The peaks and valleys of life have natural aspects to them that the desolation, the anxiety, can make us blind to. We forget that meadows are supposed to sustain life. We forget that the low valley is a natural place for growth and vegetation. It isn't easy. It doesn't feel natural, once again, but these things belong together.

The meadows and valleys are dressed in provision. They are ready to gather and be home for life and growth. Things we may not always associate with each other were made for each other.

Our seasons of desperation and stress are ready made to be seasons of slowing down. These can be times that may not feel like exotic meadow times, but we can find the opportunity to search for God. We need not feel pressure to perform or pressure to find God in a certain way. But to know, from His word, that a desolate place can become a meadow. It can become a place where we find the provision and bounty of God. We can have hope that we won't be abandoned.

***

Disappointment is a deep well. Desolation is a deep well. It is a cavern and a respite from hustle. These times, whether we are speaking of the year 2020, or other periods of loss and despair, are times to find the Lord. To experience His version and testimony of desolate places.

We don't ignore the realities; we don't pretend the pain away. But we engage, we interact and see that the Lord can restore and redeem desolate. He treats it a different way than we had previously learned to treat it.

Let us learn a new way.

Let us allow Him to touch, to come into, to heal the desolate places and the disappointments. Then, the very place we scorned will be a place of testimony.

As we encounter more in our lives that rips us apart and breaks our hearts, let us go with God into these places and let Him transform the desolation. We can experience His refreshing, His touch in a place that feels abandoned in our hearts. We can know His love and His nature in times in our lives where it seems all is lost. The more we do this, the more we allow ourselves to adopt this new pattern of seeing desolate the way He does, the more our lives are filled with testimonies of Jesus in our desolate places. The more we will come to know desolate the way He does. The truth that more can come out than what was brought in.

As our lives fill up with these testimonies, the Earth will fill up. He wants us to know Him this fully. The Earth needs us to know His heart this way. As this happens the desolate can be brought back to life.

Chapter 5

Hard seasons don't last forever. Loss softens into new things, new life. Broken hearts mend and career paths change. 2020 won't last forever. This long-awaited year will be over soon. This desolate year and wilderness time in life will end shortly. Just like all that leaves us breathless and in pain, the year and accompanying tragedies will ease their grip. The span of life we get to live is but a breath, and will make these trials seem like blips.

Our struggles and pains won't endure forever. They are not our normal. They are not life. There are sufferings for a time, and as the saying goes, "this too shall pass."

The hope isn't that we come away from pain unscathed. The goal is not that we forget and move on unharmed, unscarred.

The hope and the expectation is that we do indeed carry a scar, carry a memory, a mark that reminds us of what we survived. Something that tells the story back to us of what the Lord does every time we make it through the fire. We need tokens, memories to remind us that now is not forever.

***

Desolate for us is death, lifeless, hopeless. It's a state where we are ruled by and are bedfellows with anxiety and fear. We are marked and can see no other way of living. It's a narrative we get trapped in and think is the only narrative possible.

To us desolate carries the idea of a bitter and unavoidable end. It's a struggle daily to resist this would-be overwhelming grief.

Our God does not see desolate this way.

Jesus chose and withdrew to a desolate place for refreshment and communion. He chose a place misunderstood and even despised by His disciples to perform a miracle we will never forget, that we will never stop marveling at. He was moved with compassion for a crowd who followed Him into this desolate place. Unfazed.

Desolate wasn't an obstacle or barrier for Jesus.

In deserts and wastelands, He creates and allows rivers and waterways to erupt and overflow. He makes ways and roads through untraveled and rough terrain, to renew and restore His people. He isn't defeated by untamed and treacherous. He isn't knocked off course by the conditions around Him.

He opens a way in the desert. He splits the rocks that fall along our path. He breaks them open and we walk right through on the road that He continues to unfurl before our feet. This is His way. He removes the barriers and then He

makes them serve as a marker of His goodness and His provision. His view of desolate and barren.

He makes the desolate places, the wilderness and deserted
wastelands spring to life. He makes them partner with growth
and abundance. He brings livestock and fertile ground to the
valleys and furrows.

Psalm 65 tells us the story that God can make anything fertile ground for growth that He longs to bless and multiply.
He blesses the growth. He crowns the year.

The untamed, wild and crazy thoughts running through our
minds, the rapid heartbeats, the unknowable and frightening
future will not prevent the workings of our God to bring fertile healing ground to our lives.

These very things bow their knee to God and become healthy,
abundant soil for Him to resurrect dreams and hopes. To
bring into our bosoms the reality of who He really is. He is
a God of abundance. Our circumstances do not change His
nature.

***

We find this view that our Father wants us to share with Him,
when we get quiet. When we share space with Him, and not
only with the thoughts and fears that desolation feeds us.

We can get quiet, we can wade into the uncomfortable mo-
ments of simply sitting with His words or sitting, maybe

standing, kneeling, waiting, or breathing a few breaths with the Lord. Invite Him into the untamed. Invite Him in to review the wilderness expanding in your hearts.

It's always a challenge. What should be as natural and as unconscious as our hearts beating, has become a great effort for most of us.

Psalm 68:9 tells us "You restored your inheritance as it languished." Though we feel we are languishing, though we feel hope draining from our skin, like the color washes from our faces when we hear bad news, there is a promise of restoration.

Jeremiah 31:25, "For I will satisfy the weary soul, and every languishing soul I will replenish."

There are many promises waiting to be believed. Promises of refreshing, help and restoration in the midst of trouble, languish and desolation. All the self care in the world will not help. It will not heal the pain of living in a fallen world. No self-care can make a desolate place, a place that can produce nothing, all of a sudden overflow with life. You cannot journal enough, you cannot take enough salt baths. Netflix cannot offer you the respite desperately needed when it seems we have lost all hope. Bottles of wine will never carry the right mixture to heal the brokenness.

Desolate places hold no way through, no maps, no roads, no sources of water or sustenance. They feel aimless. They are marked by the sensation of being lost.

But our God has promised ways through the wilderness and rivers in the desert. We are not abandoned to wander. We are entreated to trust and to watch as the God who loves us, opens a fresh course of life right through the wasteland.

He makes dry places flow with water.

He makes desolate places overflow with too many leftovers.

Desolate isn't the end. It's a beginning.

About the Author:

Maranda lives in Central Oregon with her husband of nearly 14 years, and two cats. She loves to write in her spare time when she is not at work or spending time with friends. She has participated in and studied in ministry school and a church internship, as well as many other serving opportunities throughout her early years growing up in Portland, OR. During many overseas missions and ministry trips, her desire to witness God transform lives with His love has continued to grow. She is passionate about people learning that they are invited to be as close as they desire to our great knowable God. For more, follow her @marandahopewrites on Instagram, or email A Quiet Brilliance Publishing at aquietbrilliancepub@gmail.com.

Made in the USA
Monee, IL
05 October 2020